The
Corporal
and Spiritual
Works of
Mercy

The
Corporal
and Spiritual
Works of
Mercy

PONTIFICAL COUNCIL FOR THE PROMOTION
OF THE NEW EVANGELIZATION

Jubilee of Mercy
2015-2016

Our Sunday Visitor Publishing Division
Our Sunday Visitor, Inc.
Huntington, Indiana 46750

Copyright © 2015 Pontifical Council for the
Promotion of the New Evangelization
Vatican City

Published 2015 by Our Sunday Visitor
Publishing Division

20 19 18 17 16 15   1 2 3 4 5 6 7 8 9

ISBN: 978-1-61278-981-1 (Inventory No. T1741)
eISBN: 978-1-61278-989-7
LCCN: 2015951407

Translation: Damian Bacich
Cover design: Lindsey Riesen
Cover art: Shutterstock; Pontifical Council for the
Promotion of the New Evangelization
Interior design: Sherri L. Hoffman

PRINTED IN THE UNITED STATES OF AMERICA

TABLE OF CONTENTS

PREFACE

Sacred Scripture is the mirror of how mercy is expressed in its concreteness. Even before an emotional dimension, the pages of the Bible highlight the reality of mercy in its tangible and visible expression. It is with reason, then, that Pope Francis wrote in *Misericordiae Vultus* that "the mercy of God is not an abstract idea, but a concrete reality with which he reveals his love as of that of a father or a mother, moved to the very depths out of love for their child" (6).

The "great river of mercy" (*MV*, 25) never runs dry because it always finds people who give concrete testimony to it in everyday life. It is an amazing sight, which can be observed especially in times of great social and economic difficulties and in the aftermath of natural disasters: a solidarity that goes beyond language, race, religion, or country of origin. We discover that there is a sentiment that binds all men and women because we all belong to a common humanity. The corporal and spiritual works of mercy fit within this process of human solidarity and specify one of its essential features. "You did it to me" (Mt 25:40) is the unique touch that allows us to express the Christian witness.

Jesus identified himself with the hungry, the thirsty, the naked, the stranger, the sick or the imprisoned, with those who are in the grip of doubt or in distress and need help and consolation in order not to fall into anguish. At the same time, he asks us to forgive love. The second word is *raham*, the root of which denotes the love of a mother that entails kindness, tenderness, patience, understanding, and willingness to forgive. The most common Greek translation of both words and its preferential use in the New Testament is *eleos*, whence arises the liturgical invocation *"Kyrie Eleison*/Lord have mercy," as well as the word "alms" (through the Latin *eleemosyna*). In short, then, biblical mercy expresses the feeling that we experience when faced with want and misfortune, together with the action that rises from that feeling, meaning to have compassion and pity, to be moved by, to feel deep affection (like a mother), to be compassionate, love, have tender emotion, to take pity, the aid that results from a relationship of fidelity, the concrete actions it involves … (see the etymological analysis of this concept contained in the encyclical of Pope John Paul II *Dives in Misericordia*, 52).

The Old Testament: "His Mercy Endures Forever" (Ps 136)

The invocations of the psalmist never tire of repeating pleas that request mercy or compassion from the Lord (see Ps 4:2; 6:3; 9:14; 25:16; 51:1), and, in turn, thanksgiving proclamations that repeat, "Give thanks to the Lord, for he is good; for his mercy endures for ever!" (Ps 107:1), explaining this mercy that God particularly manifests in the history of the Chosen People.

The starting point of this understanding is in the earliest traditions about the call of Moses, "I have seen the affliction of my people in Egypt, and have heard their cry because of their taskmasters; I know their sufferings, and I have come down to deliver them out of the hand of the Egyptians" (Ex 3:7-8). This attitude of God arises from his fidelity to the Covenant because, "I have heard the groaning of the sons of Israel whom the Egyptians hold in bondage and I have remembered my covenant" (Ex 6:5). In his mercy God cannot stand the misery of his chosen people, since the Covenant made them "his offspring" (Acts 17:28).

In Sinai, the foundational character of God's mercy to his people is manifested in the statement, "The LORD, the LORD, a God merciful and gracious, slow to anger, and abounding in mercy and faithfulness, keeping merciful love for thousands, forgiving iniquity and transgression and sin" (Ex 34:6-7; see also Nm 14:19; Jer 3:12-14, Lam 3:22-25). In the prophetic experience such mercy takes on deep human accents when the prophet Hosea reveals that God has decided not to grant mercy to Israel and to punish it: "My heart recoils within me, my compassion grows warm and tender" (Hos 11:8). Further, "I will not execute my fierce anger ... for I am God ... I will not come to destroy" (Hos 11:9). Hence the significant way the prophet Hosea sums it up: "For I desire mercy and not sacrifice" (6:6).

Just as the prophets foretell the worst catastrophes, they also safeguard the tenderness of the heart of God as expressed emotionally by exclaiming: "Is Ephraim my dear son? / Is he my darling child? / For as often as I speak against him, / I do remember him still. / Therefore my heart yearns for him" (Jer 31:20; see also Is 49:14-15; 54:7). Israel is convinced that God's mercy touches all human experience when it asks: "Who is a God like you, pardoning iniquity and passing over transgression for the remnant of his inheritance? He does not retain his anger for ever because he delights in mercy" (Mi 7:18). Thus the cry of the psalmist remains alive when we invoke the psalm known as the *Miserere*: "Have mercy on me, O God, according to your merciful love; according to your abundant mercy blot out my transgressions" (Ps 51:1).

If God's mercy knows no limit other than the hardening of the sinner (see Is 9:16; Jer 16:5,13), after the exile the story of Jonah opens up a new universal perspective with the narrative of the closed hearts who do not accept the immense tenderness of God: "I knew that you are a gracious God and merciful, slow to anger, and abounding in mercy, and that you repent of evil" (Jon 4:2). The Book of Sirach is right when the author clearly says, "The compassion of man is for his neighbor, but the compassion of the Lord is for all living beings" (18:13). He speaks above all of the "Lord of mercy" (Wis 9:1; see also Sir 5:6; 47:22; Wis 6:6; 12:22).

The unanimous tradition of Israel is superbly collected by the psalmist in a clearly universalist perspective: "The LORD is merciful and gracious, / slow to anger and abounding in mercy. / He will not always chide, / nor will he keep his anger for ever. / He does not deal with us according to our sins, / nor repay us according to our iniquities.... / As a father pities his children, / so the LORD pities those who fear him" (Ps 103:8-13). And all this because, "with the LORD there is mercy" (Ps 130:7), since "his mercy endures forever," the liturgical invocation insistently repeated twenty times in Psalm 136!

God therefore abides by his promises and, despite man's infidelity, it is from his mercy that the final liberation from all evil is expected to come. Thus it acquires, in the history of salvation, the value of future definitive salvation, as what the Lord says to Jerusalem beautifully reminds us, "with everlasting mercy I will have compassion on you ... / For the mountains may depart / and the hills be removed, / but my mercy shall not depart from you, / and my covenant of peace shall not be removed" (Is 54:8-10; see also Jer 31:3; Micah 7:20; Ps 85:8; 90:14; 106:45; 130:7).

In the Old Testament, mercy is gradually transformed into the technical term for charitable work, "alms," designating action that brings about the good in the sense of charity, especially for the poor (see Prv 21:26; Tb 1:3; 4:5-11; Sir 7:10; 17:22; Mt 6:2; Acts 9:36).

Concrete Works and Acts of Mercy in the Old Testament

In the Book of the Prophet Isaiah there are visible acts of mercy that seem to inspire the list found in the Last Judgment of Matthew 25:35: "Is not this the fast that I choose: / to loose the bonds of wickedness, / to undo the thongs of the yoke, / to let the oppressed go free, / and to break every yoke? / Is it not to share your bread with the hungry, / and bring the homeless poor into your house; / when you see the naked, to cover him, / and not to hide yourself from your own flesh?" (Is 58:6-7).

In the Old Testament we also find the great manifesto of the prophet's mission and his works, which will serve as a presentation of Jesus's mission in Luke 4:16-21 and 7:22: "The Spirit of the Lord God is upon me, / because the Lord has anointed me / to bring good tidings to the afflicted; / he has sent me to bind up the brokenhearted, / to proclaim liberty to the captives, / and the opening of the prison to those who are bound; / to proclaim the year of the Lord's favor,/ and the day of vengeance of our God; / to comfort all who mourn" (Is 61:1-2).

With a defense of his behavior, Job remembers his own acts of benevolence: "If I have withheld anything that the poor desired, / or have caused the eyes of the widow to fail, / or have eaten my morsel alone, / and the fatherless has not eaten of it / if I have seen any one perish for lack of clothing, / or a poor man without covering / if I have raised my hand against the fatherless, / because I saw help in the gate" (Jb 31:16-17,19,21).

Even before he had refused to accept these allegations: "You have exacted pledges of your brothers for nothing, / and stripped the naked of their clothing. / You have given no water to the weary to drink, / and you have withheld bread from the hungry" (Jb 22:6-7).

Ben Sirach, the author of Ecclesiastes, recalls these works: "Stretch forth your hand to the poor, / so that your blessing may be complete. / Give graciously to all the living, / and withhold not kindness from the dead. / Do not fail those who weep, / but mourn with those who mourn. / Do not shrink from visiting a sick man, / because for such deeds you will be loved" (Sir 7:32-35). Also, "By the spirit of might he saw the last things, / and comforted those who mourned in Zion" (Sir 48:24).

And Tobias added "burying the dead" to the list: "In the days of Shalmaneser I performed many acts of charity to my brethren. I would give my bread to the hungry and my clothing to the naked; and if I saw any one of my people dead and thrown out behind the wall of Nineveh, I would bury him. And if Sennacherib the king put to death any who came fleeing from Judea, I buried them secretly. For in his anger he put many to death. When the bodies were sought by the king, they were not found" (Tb 1:16-18).

The New Testament: "Blessed Are the Merciful, for They Shall Obtain Mercy" (Mt 5:7)

In order to carry out the plan of salvation, Jesus Christ wished to be "in the likeness of men" (Phil 2:7) to experience the condition of those he wanted to save. Hence the mercy that Jesus generally witnessed to the crowds (Mt 9:36, "When he saw the crowds, he had compassion for them"; Mt 14:14, "he had compassion on them"; Mt 15:32, "Jesus ... said, 'I have compassion on the crowd' "). Luke's Gospel emphasizes more personal aspects when it evokes the "only son" of a widow (see Lk 7:12-13) or bereaved parents (Lk 8:42; 9:38,42). It also testifies to his particular goodness toward women and foreigners since "all flesh shall see the salvation of God" (Lk 3:6). Therefore, if Jesus has compassion and mercy on all, being a "merciful and faithful high priest" (Heb 2:17), we can understand how the afflicted address him with the invocation "Lord, have mercy" (Mt 17:15; see also Mt 15:22; 20:30).

God, as "Father of mercies" (2 Cor 1:3), grants mercy to Paul (see 2 Cor 4:1; 1 Tm 1:13) and promises it to other believers (Mt 5:7; 1 Tm 1:2; 2 Tm 1:2; Ti 1:4; 2 Jn 3). The perspective of mercy proper to the history of salvation is widely present in the two central canticles of Jesus' infancy according to Luke's Gospel: the first in Mary's *Magnificat* (Lk 1:50-54), and the second in the *Benedictus* of Zechariah (Lk 1:72-78). The overabundance of mercy is summed up in a paradoxical and emphatic phrase of Paul when he says, "For God has consigned all men to disobedience, that he may have mercy upon all" (Rom 11:32).

"Be merciful, even as your Father is merciful" (Lk 6:36). This is an essential condition to enter the kingdom of heaven. "Blessed are the merciful, for they shall obtain mercy" (Mt 5:7), Jesus teaches, following the words of the prophet Hosea ("For I desire mercy and not sacrifice," Hos 6:6). This tenderness should make mercy toward those who offend us possible, like the Good Samaritan (see Lk 10:30-37), since God always manifests "mercy" (Mt 18:32). Therefore, the final judgment will hinge on mercy, even unconsciously, toward Jesus through the most needy (Mt 25:31-46), because God's love is only present in those who exercise mercy. "But if any one has the world's goods and sees his brother in need, yet closes his heart against him, how does God's love abide in him?" (1 Jn 3:17).

The Paradigm of Matthew 25:31-46

This passage is a summary of doctrine and the demands of the entire Gospel, in which the brothers and sisters of the Son of man are all the needy and marginalized of our world. The text is presented as a last judgment, similar to the scenes of judgment present in apocalyptic literature (see Jl 3:1-3; Dn 7:7-27; Is 11:4), which has echoes in the New Testament (1 Cor 6:2, "the saints will judge the world"; see also Rv 20:4). These scenes are presented from the perspective of the weak and oppressed, who achieve liberation in the justice of the kingdom of God and thus reveal what the final judgment of history will be. Thus it becomes clear that the injustice of the present world is not permanent, because God's action will produce a conversion of the current established order.

The judgment is directed without distinction to all "nations" (Mt 25:32), a formulation in which the prophetic final words resound, "For I know their works and their thoughts, and I am coming to gather all nations and tongues; and they shall come and shall see my glory" (Is 66:18). Luke's closing warning also teaches us, "But watch at all times, praying that you may have strength to escape all these things that will take place, and to stand before the Son of man."(Lk 21:36). This universalist interpretation of the judgment — that is, directed to all men and women — is foretold by the Gospel of Matthew when it says, "For the Son of man is to come with his angels in the glory of his Father, and then he will repay every man for what he has done" (16:27), and says in the parable of the weeds that "the field is the world" (13:38).

We should note that this universalist interpretation of Matthew 25, whose central point is the identification of "brethren" (v. 40) with every needy human being, has been the most common one since the twentieth century and is shared by most of the specialists from various Christian confessions who have analyzed this chapter of Matthew. Concerning this universalist understanding, *Gaudium et Spes*, Vatican II's Pastoral Constitution on the Church in the Modern World, proposed Matthew 25:40 as the foundation of universal love of neighbor:

> In our times a special obligation binds us to make ourselves the neighbor of every person without exception and of actively helping him when he comes across our path, whether he be an old person abandoned by all, a foreign laborer unjustly looked down upon, a refugee, a child born of an unlawful union and wrongly suffering for a sin he did not commit, or a hungry person who disturbs our conscience by recalling the voice of the Lord, "As long as you did it for one of these the least of my brethren, you did it for me" (Mt 25:40). (27)

For its part, the *Catechism of the Catholic Church* — in addition to dealing with the works of mercy cited earlier — refers to Matthew 25 to theologically substantiate *Christ as physician* — "His compassion toward all who suffer goes so far that he identifies himself with them: 'I was sick and you visited me' " (1503) — and respect for the human person:

> The duty of making oneself a neighbor to others and actively serving them becomes even more urgent when it involves the disadvantaged, in whatever area this may be. "As you did it to one of the least of these my brethren, you did it to me." (1932)

The text of the universal judgment on the love expressed in the works of mercy is found in Matthew 25:31-46:

"When the Son of man comes in his glory, and all the angels with him, then he will sit on his glorious throne. Before him will be gathered all the nations, and he will separate them one from another as a shepherd separates the sheep from the goats, and he will place the sheep at his right hand, but the goats at the left. Then the King will say to those at his right hand, 'Come, O blessed of my Father, inherit the kingdom prepared for you from the foundation of the world; for I was hungry and you gave me food, I was thirsty and you gave me drink, I was a stranger and you welcomed me, I was naked and you clothed me, I was sick and you visited me, I was in prison and you came to me.' Then the righteous will answer him, 'Lord, when did we see you hungry and feed you, or thirsty and give you drink? And when did we see you a stranger and welcome you, or naked and clothe you? And when did we see you sick or in prison and visit you?' And the King will answer them, 'Truly, I say to you, as you did it to one of the least of these my brethren, you did it to me.' Then he will say to those at his left hand, 'Depart from me, you cursed, into the eternal fire prepared for the devil and his angels; for I was hungry and you gave me no food, I was thirsty and you gave me no drink, I was a stranger and you did not welcome me, naked and you did not clothe me, sick and in prison and you did not visit me.' Then they also will answer, 'Lord, when did we see you hungry or thirsty or a stranger or naked or sick or in prison, and did not minister to you?' Then he will answer them, 'Truly, I say to you, as you did it not to one of the least of these, you did it not to me.' And they will go away into eternal punishment, but the righteous into eternal life."

The Works Listed in Matthew 25 and Jewish Biblical Tradition

The three combinations present in Matthew 25 — I was hungry and I was thirsty / I was a stranger and naked / I was sick and in prison — gather together a tradition present in the Old Testament, particularly Isaiah 58:6-9 (chained, oppressed, hungry, homeless, naked, injured); 61:1-2 (the poor, afflicted, captives, prisoners); Job 22:6-7 (naked, hungry, thirsty); 31:17,19, 21, 31-32 (orphans, naked, poor, innocent foreigners); Tobit 1:16 -17 (hungry, naked, dead); 4:16 (hungry, naked); and Sirach 7:34-35 (afflicted, ill).

Matthew 25 also parallels the various catalogs of virtues of the New Testament regarding mercy. For example: "Have unity of spirit, sympathy, love of the brethren, a tender heart and a humble mind" (1 Pt 3:8); "He who exhorts, in his exhortation; he who contributes, in liberality; he who gives aid, with zeal; he who does acts of mercy, with cheerfulness. Rejoice with those who rejoice; weep with those who weep" (Rom 12:8,15); "Put on then, as God's chosen ones, holy and beloved, compassion, kindness, lowliness, meekness, and patience" (Col 3:12); "Remember those who are in prison, as though in prison with them; and those who are ill-treated, since you also are in the body"(Heb 13:3).

Similarly, in accounts of Jewish literature there are lists of "works of love" and "alms," bearing in mind that mercy in Rabbinic language was a technical term for charitable works as an exercise of mercy. The Rabbinic assertion of the influential *Pirkei Avot* 1:2 is significant, reflecting the tradition of 200 B.C. to A.D. 200, which states: "The world 'stands' — in such a way that it is supported solidly — on three things. Through Torah, divine service, and acts of kindness G-dliness."

With this tradition in mind, the listing of the six works of mercy present in Matthew 25 is more than a novelty. It is a development of biblical and Jewish texts. The list is particularly relevant for its poetic quality and style, in which the enumeration of the six works are divided into three pairs, forming a symbolic triptych. No wonder, then, that this text has been the bedrock of six of the seven corporal works of mercy in the Christian tradition, to which "bury the dead" was later added," taken from Tobit 1:17 in order to achieve the number seven, the number of fullness. Thomas Aquinas justifies such action with the witness of Tobias and the disciples who buried Jesus in the tomb (see *Summa Theologica* II-II, q. 32, 2, ad 1).

Christ's Identification with "the Least of My Brethren"

The issue of Christ's identification with the "least" of his brethren as the object of the works of love and mercy is extremely relevant. Such orientation is applied to God in the Old Testament in a pointed way — "He who is kind to the poor lends to the Lord, and he will repay him for his deed" (Prv 19:17) — and it resonated in Vatican II when it said, "It is as if Christ himself were crying out in these poor to beg the charity of the disciples" (*Gaudium et Spes*, 88).

In the Gospels, we find such identification when Jesus says, "He who hears you hears me, and he who rejects you rejects me, and he who rejects me rejects him who sent me" (Lk 10:16). That axiom is certainly behind the statements identifying Matthew 25:40, "you did it to me," and Matthew 25:45, "you did it not to me," and it resounds in, "I tell you, every one who acknowledges me before men, the Son of man also will acknowledge before the angels of God; but he who denies me before men will be denied before the angels of God" (Lk 12:8-9). Later, Luke presents the exalted Lord saying to Paul, persecutor of the followers of Jesus, "Why do you persecute me?" (Acts 9:4; 22:7; 26:14).

And within the same Gospel of Matthew we find the parallel most closely related to this identification in the clear statement: "He who receives you receives me, and he who receives me receives him who sent me. And whoever gives to one of these little ones even a cup of cold water because he is a disciple, truly, I say to you, he shall not lose his reward" (Mt 10:40,42).

Sts. Cyprian and Augustine discussed this identification in order to provoke the practice of the works of mercy, with the idea of meeting the Lord through the indigent, "he who pays no attention to suffering, despises the Lord present in him" (Cyprian, *On Works and Alms*, 23), and "everyone hopes to find Christ sitting in heaven; but look, he is lying in the portal, see him in the hungry, in the one who is cold, in the one who has nothing, in the foreigner" (Augustine, *Sermon 25*, 8). The Rule of St. Benedict (fifth century) also assumes this identification, "Let all guests who arrive be received like Christ, for he is going to say, 'I came as a guest, and you received me'" (53.1).

Pope Paul VI, in his encyclical *Mysterium Fidei* (1965), introduced the newness of the presence of Christ in the neediest by citing Matthew 25:40, when he offers an overview of the various modes of Christ's presence in the Church. Echoing the forms of presence that Vatican II's *Sacrosanctum Concilium* offers (two or three are gathered in prayer, the pilgrim Church, the preaching of the Gospel, the governance of the Church, the Sacrament of the Eucharist most sublimely [see 7]), he incorporates the presence of Christ in the needy in a new way: "He is present in the Church as she performs her works of mercy, not just because whatever good we do to one of His least brethren we do to Christ himself, but also because Christ is the one who performs these works through the Church and who continually helps men with His divine love" (35).

Unity of Love of Neighbor with Love of God in Christianity

Note that in Matthew 25:31-46, the criterion for judgment is love, in accord with Jesus' preaching in the Gospel of Matthew, where he proclaimed love as the supreme commandment: "For if you love those who love you, what reward have you? Do not even the tax collectors do the same?" (see 5:21-48). "Teacher, which is the great commandment in the law?" (22:34-40). No wonder St. John of the Cross, in a classic quote, comments, "As we prepare to leave this life, we will be judged on the basis of love" (*Sayings of Light and Love*, 57, cited in *Misericordiae Vultus*, 15).

In this context, we should note the anonymity of identification with Christ that shines the triple question: "Lord, when did we see you hungry and feed you, or thirsty and give you drink? And when did we see you a stranger and welcome you, or naked and clothe you? And when did we see you sick or in prison and visit you?" (Mt 25:37-39; repeated negatively in verse 44). On this sensitive issue, which should be understood in a theologically correct way, Vatican II provides two fundamental passages:

Those also can attain to salvation who through no fault of their own do not know the Gospel of Christ or his Church, yet sincerely seek God and moved by grace strive by their deeds to do his will as it is known to them through the dictates of conscience. Nor does Divine Providence deny the helps necessary for salvation to those who, without blame on their part, have not yet arrived at an explicit knowledge of God and with his grace strive to live a good life. Whatever good or truth is found amongst them is looked upon by the Church as a preparation for the Gospel. She knows that it is given by him who enlightens all men so that they may finally have life. (*Lumen Gentium*, 16)

Also:

All this holds true not only for Christians, but for all men of good will in whose hearts grace works in an unseen way. For, since Christ died for all men, and since the ultimate vocation of man is in fact one, and divine, we ought to believe that the Holy Spirit in a manner known only to God offers to every man the possibility of being associated with this paschal mystery. (*Gaudium et Spes*, 22).

The idea of the anonymous identification with Christ should be understood as applying to persons of "good will." Thus, according to the description in *Lumen Gentium*, it refers to those who "sincerely seek God and moved by grace strive by their deeds to do his will as it is known to them through the dictates of conscience" and "those who, without blame on their part, have not yet arrived at an explicit knowledge of God and with His grace strive to live a good life." Note, however, that in no way does it suggest that in these cases salvation is achieved by a merely "natural philanthropy," because the very conciliar text quoted here recalls that salvation is achieved by the grace of God. It would also contradict *Lumen Gentium*, which stresses "the necessity of faith and baptism" [see Mk 16:16; Jn 3:5], and "also the necessity of the Church" (*LG*, 14).

In short, then, it is "people who truly love and that are gifted with the Spirit of truth in a way that is hidden from us," as Hans Urs von Balthasar said; who are "hidden saints," according to St. Augustine; "Christians in hope," in Karl Barth's term; "latent Church," as philosopher Paul Tillich said; or "anonymous Christians," considering that "it would be a mistake to think that the latter term — the term is not what matters — would reduce the importance of mission, of preaching, baptism. What this thesis states, furthermore, was taught objectively by Vatican II in *Lumen Gentium* 16," in Karl Rahner's explanation.

Thus the Christian unity of love of neighbor with love of God becomes visible, since "on these two commandments depend all the law and the prophets" (Mt 22:40). Bearing in mind, "No man has ever seen God; if we love one another, God abides in us and his love is perfected in us" (1 Jn 4:12). Thus "he who does not love his brother whom he has seen, cannot love God whom he has not seen" (1 Jn 4:20). Hence the significance of loving one's neighbor for the knowledge of God, something particularly important for the people of our modern world, so long as this love of neighbor is radical and without reservation, since only in this way can it implicitly refer to Christ (see Mt 25:40-45) and not fall into what Paul denounces, "If I give away all I have, and if I deliver my body to be burned, but have not love, I gain nothing" (1 Cor 13:3; see also Mk 8:36). This all points out that you can give everything you have to the poor and lack love, the condition without which there can be no Christian life!

Testimonies from Tradition on Matthew 25
and the Works of Mercy

Initial lists of works of mercy

In the middle of the second century, Hermas presented the list of twenty "good works" that specify the way of living relationships with others to which the Christian is called:

> Minister to widows, to visit the orphans and the needy, to ransom the servants of God from their afflictions, to be hospitable (for in hospitality benevolence from time to time has a place), to resist no man, to be tranquil, to show yourself more submissive than all men, to reverence the aged, to practice righteousness, to observe brotherly feeling, to endure injury, to be long-suffering, to bear no grudge, to exhort those who are sick at soul, not to cast away those that have stumbled from the faith, but to convert them and to put courage into them, to reprove sinners, not to oppress debtors and indigent persons. (*Shepherd of Hermas*, Mand. VIII, 38:10)

For his part, Irenaeus of Lyons (second century), often commented on Matthew 25 and argued that when you give something to the needy it is given to God and stressed its parallel with Proverbs 19:17:

> For even as God does not need our possessions, so do we need to offer something to God; as Solomon says: "He that has pity upon the poor, lends unto the Lord" [Prv 19:17]. For God, who stands in need of nothing, takes our good works to himself for this purpose, that he may grant us a recompense of his own good things, as Our Lord says: "Come, you blessed of My Father, receive the kingdom prepared for you. For I was [hungry], and you gave

Me to eat: I was thirsty, and you gave Me drink: I was a stranger, and you took Me in: naked, and you clothed Me; sick, and you visited Me; in prison, and you came to Me [Mt 25:34-36]." (*Against Heresies*, Book 4, Chapter 18:6)

Subsequently, Origen (d. 254) opened the way to the spiritual works of mercy in a new way, true to his allegorical exegesis of Matthew 25:34-46, as follows:

In addition to bread and clothing serving the body, souls should be fed with spiritual food ... with the lining of various virtues by teaching doctrine to minister to one's neighbor with a heart full of virtues, and finally to dedicate oneself to the weak to comfort them, teaching them, consoling or rebuking them; and each of these gestures is done towards Christ. (*In Matthaeum*, 72)

Cyprian of Carthage (d. 258), wrote a short treatise on *Good Works and Almsgiving* and indicates two classic biblical texts on the actions of mercy, the aforementioned Tobit 1:16-18, which focused on alms and burial of the dead, and Isaiah 58:6-9, which mentioned the chained, oppressed, hungry, homeless, naked, and wounded (see *De Dominica oratione 32*).

Subsequently, Lactantius (d.c. 320) presents a list similar to the one that would later be enshrined in tradition, with a notable emphasis on the new classification of these actions as "works of mercy":

If any one is in need of food, let us bestow it; if any one meets us who is naked, let us clothe him; if any one suffers injury from one who is more powerful than himself, let us rescue him. Let our house be open to strangers, or to those who are in need of shelter. Let our defense not be wanting to wards, or our protection to the defenseless. To ransom captives is a great work of pity, and also to visit and comfort the sick who are in poverty. If the helpless or strangers die, we should not permit them to lie unburied. These are the works, these the duties, of pity; and if any one undertakes these, he will offer unto God a true and acceptable sacrifice. (*Epitome*, 65, 6)

St. John Chrysostom (c. 349-407) is significant because he is considered the driving force behind the formulation of the "sacrament of the brother" (especially among the Orthodox, such as Skobtsova and Clement, but also Catholics such as von Balthasar, Congar, and Tillard). In his commentary on Matthew 25 he relates it to the Eucharist evocatively in a classic text:

Would you do honor to Christ's body? Neglect him not when naked; do not while here you honor him with silken garments, neglect him perishing without of cold and nakedness. For he that said, "This is my body," and by his word confirmed the fact, this same said, "You saw me an hungered, and fed me not"; and, "Inasmuch as you did it not to one of the least of these, you did it not to me" [Mt 25:31-46]....

Even so do thou honor him with this honor, which he ordained, spending your wealth on poor people. (*Homily 50 on Matthew*, 4)

St. Augustine (354-430) also discussed the six prescribed works in Matthew 25, confirming the parallel between the two forms of works of mercy, corporal and spiritual. This division, from Augustine on, would eventually become traditional:

Not only, then, the man who gives food to the hungry, drink to the thirsty, clothing to the naked, hospitality to the stranger, shelter to the fugitive, who visits the

sick and the imprisoned, ransoms the captive, assists the
weak, leads the blind, comforts the sorrowful, heals the
sick, puts the wanderer on the right path, gives advice to
the perplexed, and supplies the wants of the needy — not
this man only, but the man who pardons the sinner also
gives alms. (*Handbook on Faith, Hope, and Love*, 72:19)

And in other texts he confirms that "there are two ways of
mercy: give and forgive. Give the good you have and forgive the evil
that is received" (*Sermon 42*:1; see *City of God* XXI:22).

In the same vein, St. Gregory the Great (d. 604) also "spiritu-
ally" interpreted the four merciful actions in Job 29:12: "I delivered
the poor supplicant, the orphan without a defender; I received the
blessing of the dying, relieved the heart of the widow."

But it was not until Peter Comestor (d. 1178), commenting on
Matthew 25, that the reference to "bury the dead" is incorporated,
probably for the first time, taken from Tobit 1:17; 2:4; 12:12 (see
In Evangelia, 45), thus following the preference of the historical
moment for seven as an expression of completeness (the seven sac-
raments, the seven deadly sins, etc.). In this context, the sevenfold
number of the works of mercy would become widespread, facilitat-
ing memorization with the use of seven Latin verbs: *visito, poto, cibo,
redimo, tego, colligo, condo*, indicating the corporal works, together
with seven other verbs: *consule, carpe, done, solare, remitte, fer, ora*, to
mark the spiritual works.

The Consolidation of the Double List of Works of Mercy in Thomas Aquinas

With Thomas Aquinas (1225-1274) the double list is theologically consolidated. On the one hand, there are the *seven corporal
works of mercy*, six from Matthew 25 and the burial of the dead
attested to in Tobit. On the other hand, as an allegorical reading of
these, he presents the *seven spiritual works*, which through him are
widely disseminated. The theological justification of this double list

pertaining to mercy show that it arises from charity, because "mercy is the greatest virtue," which gives it an innovative doctrinal richness and evangelical motivation, to which prior theologians were not as sensitive (see *Summa Theologica* II-II, Q.23, aa. 2-3).

CHAPTER TWO

The Corporal Works of Mercy

Each of the seven corporal works of mercy remedies a deficiency in our neighbor. Indeed, in his body, a person can experience a consistent lack of resources, whether internal (first: food; second: drink), or external (third: clothing; fourth: shelter), or suffering (fifth: disease; sixth: imprisonment; seventh: burial). The traditional seven works of mercy known as "corporal" respond to these (Noye, 1980). Here are some brief notes on each of them.

Feed the Hungry

First Work of Mercy in Matthew 25:35

"Give us this day our daily bread" (Mt 6:11), says the Lord's Prayer (see Mt 6:9-13; Lk 11:1-4). The basic food in Palestine during Jesus' day was bread, so the normal act of taking food was indicated by the expression to eat bread (Gn 37:25). Such importance is reflected in the name of God, to whom the request for bread is directed, "he who gives food to all flesh" (Ps 136:25) as if bread were missing, all is missing (Am 4:6; Gn 28:20).

Hunger is characteristic of the wilderness experience of God's people so well expressed in this way: "And you shall remember all the way which the LORD your God has led you these forty years in the wilderness, that he might humble you, testing you to know what was in your heart, whether you would keep his commandments, or not. And he humbled you and let you hunger and fed you with manna" (Dt 8:2-3). This dramatic experience helps us to understand the significance of this prophetic utterance, " 'Behold, the days are coming,' says the Lord GOD, / 'when I will send a famine on the land; / not a famine of bread, nor a thirst for water, / but of hearing the words of the LORD" (Am 8:11).

Among the foods of the desert, bread has many symbolic meanings. In the first place, manna, described as "bread of heaven" and "the food of angels" (Ps 78:24; Wis 16:20). And, in turn, it is seen as a symbol of the Word of the Lord (see Dt 8:3; Is 55:2,6,11), of the teachings of wisdom (Prv 9:5), and "wisdom" itself (Sir 15:3; see also 24:19-20).

On the other hand, hunger is characteristic of the poor, whom Jesus proclaims blessed for such "hunger" and because they yearn for "righteousness" (Mt 5:6). Jesus' answer to the first temptation, taken from Deuteronomy 8:3, resonates well here, "Man shall not live by bread alone, / but by every word that proceeds from the mouth of God" (Mt 4:4; see also Lk 4:4).

For its part, the Letter of James, responding to the problems of the early Church, leaves a very enlightening text when it says: "What does it profit, my brethren, if a man says he has faith but has not works? Can his faith save him? If a brother or sister is poorly clothed and in lack of daily food, and one of you says to them, "Go in peace, be warmed and filled," without giving them the things needed for the body, what does it profit? So faith by itself, if it has no works, is dead" (2:14-17).

A passage from Pope Benedict XVI's encyclical *Caritas in Veritate* can serve as a synthesis since it makes the work of mercy "feed the hungry" a responsibility of the Church coming from the very action of Jesus of Nazareth:

Life in many poor countries is still extremely insecure as a consequence of food shortages, and the situation could become worse: hunger still reaps enormous numbers of victims among those who, like Lazarus, are not permitted to take their place at the rich man's table, contrary to the hopes expressed by Paul VI. Feed the hungry (cf. Mt 25:35,37,42) is an ethical imperative for the universal Church, as she responds to the teachings of her Founder, the Lord Jesus, concerning solidarity and the sharing of goods. Moreover, the elimination of world hunger has also, in the global era, become a requirement for safeguarding the peace and stability of the planet. Hunger is not so much dependent on lack of material things as on shortage of social resources, the most important of which are institutional.... The right to food, like the right to water, has an important place within the pursuit of other rights, beginning with the fundamental right to life. It is therefore necessary to cultivate a public conscience that considers food and access to water as universal rights of all human beings, without distinction or discrimination. (27)

In short, since hunger is the symbol of the need for real food, the Gospel of John states that Jesus alone can satisfy it, being himself "the bread of life" (Jn 6:35). Moreover, it is instructive that since its inception the Eucharistic celebration has its center in the breaking of bread that is handed over ("breaking of the bread": Lk 24:35, Acts 2:42). It is an expression of the fact that the Eucharist starts from Jesus' gesture of sharing and giving, "And he took bread, and when he had given thanks he broke it and gave it to them, saying, 'This is my body which is given for you' " (Lk 22:19). Thus the Sacrament of the Eucharist is significantly characterized by Vatican II as the source and summit of all Christian life (see *Lumen Gentium*, 11).

Give Drink to the Thirsty

Second Work of Mercy in Matthew 25:35

"After this Jesus, knowing that all was now finished, said (to fulfil the Scripture), 'I thirst' " (Jn 19:28). His thirst, terrible for those facing the torment of the cross, recalls the mortal anguish of Psalm 69:21: "They gave me gall for food, / and for my thirst they gave me vinegar to drink." It also has a deeper meaning linked to Jesus' ardent desire to return to the Father according to the invocation of the psalmist: "O God ... my soul thirsts for you" (Ps 63:1); "My soul thirsts for God, / for the living God. / When shall I come and behold / the face of God?" (Ps 42:2). These resonate with the emphatic request, "Give me a drink!" (Jn 4:7), spoken to the Samaritan woman by Jesus.

In the Bible, water also contains a symbolic meaning. The water that came from the rock in the desert signifies God's gift to His chosen people (see Ex 17:1-7; Nm 20:1-13). Water also becomes a symbol of God himself, in the beautiful prayer of Psalm 42:2: "As a deer longs / for flowing streams, / so longs my soul / for you, O God." The prophetic text of Jeremiah 2:13 also touches on this: "They have forsaken me, / the fountain of living waters" (see also Is 12:2-3; Jer 17:13).

In the New Testament, we are reminded that apostolic ministry comprises trials and tribulations, among which is "hunger and thirst" (1 Cor 4:11; 2 Cor 11:27). Therefore, giving even just a glass of water to the disciples sent by the Lord is a gesture that will not be forgotten by him (see Mt 10:42; Mk 9:41). It is not surprising, in this context, that hope of liberation is formulated in these clear terms: "They shall hunger no more, neither thirst any more; / the sun shall not strike them, nor any scorching heat" (Rv 7:16).

It is thus important that the symbolism of water finds its full meaning in Christian baptism. Just as water purifies, so does baptism, "not as a removal of dirt from the body but as an appeal to God for a clear conscience, through the resurrection of Jesus Christ"

(1 Pt 3:21). Baptism is thus conceived as "the washing of regeneration and renewal in the Holy Spirit" (Ti 3:5; see also Jn 3:5). The Sacrament of Baptism may also be seen symbolically announced in the "water" that came out of the side of Jesus crucified (Jn 19:34), according to the interpretation of many Fathers and relevant theologians (in particular St. Augustine and St. Thomas Aquinas), a perspective taken up by *Lumen Gentium* 3 when dealing with the beginning of the Church.

The issue of water and thirst appears significantly in the Message to the People of God of the 2012 Synod of Bishops, which focused on "the New Evangelization for the Transmission of the Christian Faith." The bishops describe the present moment, beginning with the Samaritan woman's exclamation, "Sir, give me this water, that I may not thirst, nor come here to draw" (Jn 4:15). The beginning of this Message to the People of God says:

> Let us draw light from a Gospel passage: Jesus' encounter with the Samaritan woman (cf. Jn 4:5-42). There is no man or woman who, in one's life, would not find oneself like the woman of Samaria beside a well with an empty bucket, with the hope of finding the fulfillment of the heart's most profound desire, that which alone could give full meaning to life. Today, many wells offer themselves up in order to quench humanity's thirst, but we must discern in order to avoid polluted waters. We must orient the search well, so as not to fall prey to disappointment, which can be damaging.
>
> Like Jesus at the well of Sychar, the Church also feels the need to sit beside today's men and women. She wants to render the Lord present in their lives so that they can encounter him because his Spirit alone is the water that gives true and eternal life. Only Jesus can read the depths of our heart and reveal the truth about ourselves: "He told me everything I have done,"

the woman confesses to her fellow citizens. This word of proclamation is united to the question that opens up to faith: "Could he possibly be the Messiah?" It shows that whoever receives new life from encountering Jesus cannot but proclaim truth and hope to others. The sinner who was converted becomes a messenger of salvation and leads the whole city to Jesus. The people pass from welcoming her testimony to personally experiencing the encounter: "We no longer believe because of your word; for we have heard for ourselves, and we know that this is truly the savior of the world." (1)

To conclude this work of mercy — complementary to the previous one, "feed the hungry" — it is also good to remember a passage from the latest encyclical of Pope Francis, *Laudato Si'*, that deals with the issue of water. To begin his reflection, the pope notes with clarity that entire peoples, and especially children, fall ill and die from drinking unsafe water, while pollution of water tables due to discharges made by factories and cities continues. For this reason, the he states:

> Yet access to safe drinkable water is a basic and universal human right, since it is essential to human survival and, as such, is a condition for the exercise of other human rights. Our world has a grave social debt towards the poor who lack access to drinking water, because they are denied the right to a life consistent with their inalienable dignity. (30)

Clothe the Naked

Fourth Work of Mercy in Matthew 25:36

No other saint has entered into popular memory like St. Martin of Tours, with his mantle divided and donated to a beggar. The most famous tradition around his life takes place in the winter of 337, when Martin meets a shivering beggar near the city gate, to whom he gives half of his cloak (the other half belongs to the Roman army in which he is serving). The following night, Christ appears to Martin, wearing half of the cloak, to thank him. No doubt it is a concrete realization of the work of mercy praised in Matthew 25:36, as Martin did not know that in the poor beggar he was meeting Christ himself.

In the Bible, nakedness is negative, seen as a result of sin (see Gn 3:7), and as that of a slave being sold (Gn 37:23), of the imprisoned (Is 20:4; Acts 12:8), and of the mentally ill living in conditions of alienation (Mk 5:1-20). Indeed, the nakedness of the marginalized is particularly humiliating, as told in the Book of Job speaking of the poor, "They lie all night naked, without clothing, / and have no covering in the cold…. / They go about naked, without clothing; / hungry" (24:7-10).

The Bible suggests an attitude of compassion toward nakedness in counseling, "Give of your bread to the hungry, and of your clothing to the naked" (Tb 4:16); praising the one who "covers the naked with a garment" (Ez 18:16); and advising, "when you see the naked, to cover him" (Is 58:7). Therefore, in Matthew 25:36, such action is seen as a work of mercy.

In contrast to nakedness, in the Bible, clothing is a sign of the spiritual condition of man, and the color white particularly indicates eschatological salvation, marking those beings associated with God (see Eccl 9:8; Sir 43:18). The Book of Revelation, in its description of the heavenly world, most insistently emphasizes these characteristics (2:17; 14:14), already present throughout the Bible to describe beings from heaven (Ez 9:2; Dn 7:9; Rv 1:13). In this context, the contrast between the naked young man in Mark 14:51, a symbol of the death of Jesus, and the young man "dressed in a white robe" in Mark 16:5, who announces the resurrection of Jesus Christ, concretely suggests the deeper meaning of "clothe the naked" in Matthew 25:36, since by believing in the Resurrection the young man dresses (in white!) as a sign of his hope fulfilled!

The Pauline tradition also strongly emphasizes that nakedness is an expression of the "old man" disappearing thanks to having "put on the new man, who is being renewed in knowledge after the image of his creator" (Col 3:10; see also Eph 4:24). This happens through faith and baptism by which you "have put on Christ" (Gal 3:27), bearing in mind that even nakedness "shall separate us from the love of Christ" (Rom 8:35), since "we would be unclothed, but that we would be further clothed, so that what is mortal may be swallowed up by life" (2 Cor 5:4).

Welcome the Stranger

The Third Work of Mercy in Mattthew 25:35

The words of Matthew 25:35, "I was a stranger and you welcomed me," marked the history of Israel. In effect, the visitor who comes and asks for the shelter he lacks reminds Israel of its past condition as a sojourner and foreigner passing through the world, as witnessed in these texts: "The stranger who sojourns with you shall be to you as the native among you, and you shall love him as yourself; for you were strangers in the land of Egypt" (Lv 19:34); "Hear my prayer, O LORD, / and give ear to my cry; / hold not your peace at my tears! / For I am your passing guest, / a sojourner, like all my fathers" (Ps 39:12); "Therefore let us go forth to him outside the camp.... For here we have no lasting city, but we seek the city which is to come" (Heb 13:13-14).

This stranger needs to be welcomed and treated with love, in the name of the God who loves him ("loves the sojourner": Dt 10:18). He must be defended against great difficulties (see Gn 19.8), and we should not hesitate to trouble our friends if we do not have the means to help an unexpected stranger (Lk 11:5).

An example of generous and religious welcome is Abraham with the three personages in Mamre, a paradigm of all hospitality (see Gn 18:1-8), and Job who boasts of it (Jb 31:31). Christ himself approves of the care welcoming the stranger entails (Lk 7:44-46) and who, in turn, is welcomed into the home of the disciples of Emmaus who recognize him precisely in the breaking of bread (Lk 24:13-33). All these gestures of welcoming the stranger are concrete manifestations of "let love be genuine, practice hospitality" (Rom 12:9,13).

Within the Christian tradition the Rule of St. Benedict particularly stands out. It calls the monks to practice hospitality with this statement, reminiscent of Matthew 25:40: "Let all guests who arrive be received like Christ, for He is going to say, 'I came as a guest, and you received me' " (53.1). It also describes how the monks must interact with the guests: "In the salutation of all guests, whether arriving or departing, let all humility be shown. Let the head be bowed or the whole body prostrated on the ground in adoration of Christ, who indeed is received in their persons" (53.6).

Visit the Sick

Fifth Work of Mercy in Matthew 25:36

"Illness and suffering have always been among the gravest problems confronted in human life. In illness, man experiences his powerlessness, his limitations, and his finitude. Every illness can make us glimpse death" (*Catechism of the Catholic Church*, 1500).

The sick man par excellence in the Old Testament is Job, who asks his friends to harken to him: "Hear now my reasoning, / and listen to the pleadings of my lips" (Jb 13:6). He later repeats, "Listen carefully to my words, / and let this be your consolation" (21:2).

Testimony about the act of visiting the sick, not very common in the Bible, is described by Ben Sirach as an act of love for the visitor: "Do not shrink from visiting a sick man, / because for such deeds you will be loved" (Sir 7:35). This text expresses the Jewish understanding which emphasizes the visitor and not the sick, in contrast to Matthew 25:36, where it is the sick person who has a dignity that must be recognized because it is Christ himself!

In this sense, "the sick person has a Christic sacramentality which makes him into a sacrament of Christ" (Manicardi). Such a perspective requires the visitor to discover in his encounter with the poor and disabled sick person a path and an interpretation that can lead to an identification with Christ who "though he was rich, yet for your sake he became poor" (2 Cor 8:9).

In the New Testament, there appears a standard form of visiting the sick, made up of three moments: visit, prayer, and ritual, the latter having two forms (the imposition of hands or anointing with oil). Thus Luke tells of Paul's visit to the home of Publius: "It happened that the father of Publius lay sick with fever and dysentery; and Paul visited him and prayed, and putting his hands on him healed him" (Acts 28:8). And James explains that priests should be called when one is sick: "Is any among you sick? Let him call for the elders of the church, and let them pray over him, anointing him with oil in the name of the Lord; and the prayer of faith will save the sick man, and the Lord will raise him up; and if he has committed sins, he will be forgiven" (Jas 5:14-15).

The latter text has been considered by Christian tradition as the basis and the biblical root of the Sacrament of the Anointing of the Sick, hinted at in the mission of the Twelve in which they "anointed with oil many that were sick and healed them" (Mk 6:13). Vatican II explains the sacrament in this way:

> By the sacred anointing of the sick and the prayer of her priests the whole Church commends the sick to the suffering and glorified Lord, asking that he may lighten their suffering and save them; she exhorts them, moreover, to contribute to the welfare of the whole people of God by associating themselves freely with the passion and death of Christ. (*Lumen Gentium*, 11)

It should be noted that it was not until the eleventh century that this sacrament acquired the name "extreme unction," since it occurs after the anointing (or unction) of the Christian in baptism and confirmation, and gradually led to its understanding in practice as the "sacrament of death" about the fifteenth century. The Council of Trent preferred to speak of "extreme unction" as "the completion of the whole Christian life," although it also used the name "anointing of the sick." For its part, the Vatican II prescribed a return to calling it "anointing of the sick," rather than "extreme unction" because it "is not a sacrament for those only who are at the point of death" (*Sancrosanctum Concilium*, 73).

Visit the Imprisoned

Sixth Work of Mercy in Matthew 25:36

In the background of this work of mercy lie those emblematic places in the Bible that announce liberation to prisoners, such as, "proclaim release to the captives" (Lk 4:18), evoking the phrase "proclaim liberty to the captives" in Isaiah 61:1. We are called to remember those in prison as if they were our cellmates — "Remember those who are in prison, as though in prison with them" (Heb 13:3) — and hear the fundamental words of Jesus, "I was in prison and you came to me" (Mt 25:36).

No wonder, then, that in the New Testament there is a special relationship between the members of the Christian communities and the brethren imprisoned for reasons of faith, as recalled by the saying of Jesus that "they will lay their hands on you and persecute you, delivering you up to the synagogues and prisons" (Lk 21:12). In this context, the Letter to the Hebrews states, "You had compassion on the prisoners, and you joyfully accepted the plundering of your property, since you knew that you yourselves had a better possession and an abiding one" (10:34).

Important examples include the proximity of the community through intercessory prayer to Peter who was imprisoned: "So Peter was kept in prison; but earnest prayer for him was made to God by the Church" (Acts 12:5). For his part, Paul expresses his gratitude for the closeness of Christians in Philippi during his detention, as well as the aid he received (see Phil 1:13,17; 2:25; 4:15-18).

Obviously pastoral care to prisoners should also focus on their families, supporting them so they can best assist the prisoners.... Forms of Christian presence in prisons are multiple and creative. Ultimately, "to visit the imprisoned" cannot be separated from political work and reflection which, in the name of human dignity and human rights, try to envision forms of punishment that do not deprive one of freedom, but which require acts of reparation. (Manicardi)

Bury the Dead

Seventh Work of Mercy in Tobit 1:17 and 12:12

In Israel, to be deprived of burial was seen as a horrible evil (see Ps 79:3), which was part of the punishment with which the wicked were threatened (1 Kgs 14:11-13; Jer 22:18-19). So, it was a work of piety and pious practice in Judaism. Hence the exhortations of Ben Sirach: "Withhold not kindness from the dead" (Sir 7:33) and "My son, let your tears fall for the dead, / and as one who is suffering grievously begin the lament. / Lay out his body with the honor due him, / and do not neglect his burial" (Sir 38:16).

The Book of Tobit provides the relevant testimony of this practice:

In the days of Shalmaneser I performed many acts of charity to my brethren. I would give my bread to the hungry and my clothing to the naked; and if I saw any one of my people dead and thrown out behind the wall of Nineveh, I would bury him. And if Sennacherib the king put to death any who came fleeing from Judea, I buried them secretly. (1:16-18)

And so, when you and your daughter-in-law Sarah prayed, I brought a reminder of your prayer before the

Holy One; and when you buried the dead, I was likewise present with you. (12:12)

Tobias, therefore, includes the good work of "burying the dead" after the works of mercy "feed the hungry" and "clothe the naked." This joint list is what possibly influenced its inclusion with the last six listed after Matthew 25.

A deeper reason for such inclusion is that given by St. Thomas Aquinas. On the one hand, he stresses that the silence about burial in the first six works of mercy is because the former are "more clearly necessary" and, on the other hand, indicates that "it does concern the deceased what is done with his body: both that he may live in the memory of man whose respect he forfeits if he remain without burial, and as regards a man's fondness for his own body while he was yet living, a fondness which kindly persons should imitate after his death. It is thus that some are praised for burying the dead, as Tobias, and those who buried Our Lord" (*Summa Theoligica*, II-II, q. 32, a.2, ad 1).

This explicit reference to the burial of Jesus gives the key to understanding this work of mercy because, again according to Thomas, "by Christ's rising from the grave, to them who are in the grave, hope is given of rising again through Him, according to John 5:25-28" (*Summa*, III, q. 51,1). Thus the oldest Easter confession linking the death and resurrection of Jesus includes a reference to burial — Holy Saturday — as the confirmation of death, which, in turn, thanks to Christ risen from the tomb, is the path to resurrection (see 1 Cor 15:3-5).

And what about cremation? Since 1963, an instruction of the Congregation for the Doctrine of the Faith indicates that the Catholic Church, while maintaining its traditional preference for burial, agrees to accompany those who have chosen cremation unless it is done for explicitly anti-Christian motives (see also Code of Canon Law, 1176). Hence the importance of taking particular care with the corresponding liturgical celebration!

This new practice of cremation, in turn, invites reflection on the profound question for every human person that is dead, aware, however, that the Christian faith, "affirms that a spiritual element survives and subsists after death, an element endowed with consciousness and will, so that the 'human self' subsists. To designate this element, the Church uses the word 'soul,' the accepted term in the usage of Scripture and Tradition. Although not unaware that this term has various meanings in the Bible, the Church thinks that there is no valid reason for rejecting it" (Congregation for the Doctrine of the Faith, *Note on Certain Questions Concerning Eschatology*, 1979, 3).

In short, then, it is faith in the immortality of the "person," or human self (or soul), which survives as such transformed by the saving action of God in Jesus Christ, when God will be "everything to every one" (1 Cor 15:28), in "a new heaven and a new earth" (Rv 21:1) where "death shall be no more, neither shall there be mourning nor crying nor pain" (Rv 21:4)!

CHAPTER THREE

The Spiritual Works of Mercy

Human persons suffer deficiencies in their spiritual dimension, to which the spiritual works of mercy respond, either by imploring the help of God (seventh: prayer), intervening by instructing or advising others (second: treats deficiencies through teaching; first: provides counsel), comforting (fourth: in suffering and sadness), or by reacting to the disorders of their action (third: admonishing; fifth: forgiving; sixth: bearing with them). The spiritual works of mercy are therefore more valuable than material aid, although there are situations in which the latter is more urgent (Noye, 1980).

From their beginnings these seven spiritual works of mercy, unlike the seven corporal works of mercy, were entrusted to each individual and therefore proposed as a general rule to each and every Christian to put into practice. Their development began in the patristic period, particularly with Origen, beginning with his allegorical interpretation of the text of Matthew 25. Augustine followed this same line, which was consecrated in a particular way in the thirteenth century in the academic world, especially with St. Thomas Aquinas.

These seven spiritual works of mercy can be grouped into three blocks. First are the three initial works of vigilance: 1) counsel the doubtful; 2) instruct the ignorant; 3) admonish sinners. Then there are three central works focused on reconciliation: 4) comforting the afflicted; 5) forgiving offenses willingly; 6) bearing wrongs patiently. Finally is the work that sums up the others: 7) prayer, focused on asking God on behalf of the living and the dead (Keenan, 2008). What follows is a brief note on each of them.

Be Watchful

The practice of the three spiritual works of mercy that fit under this category — counsel the doubtful, instruct the ignorant, and admonish sinners — teaches us to look outside of ourselves. It invites us to a new watchfulness made of compassion and love for those in need, ignorant, or in error.

Counsel the Doubtful

Biblical tradition stresses the importance of counsel: "In an abundance of counselors there is safety" (Prv 11:14); "The knowledge of a wise man will increase like a flood, / and his counsel like a flowing spring" (Sir 21:13); "Those who are wise shall shine like the brightness of the firmament" (Dn 12:3).

But where is the criterion for good counsel? Here are the words of the sage Ben Sirach which point out the issue of truth and the critical importance of good conscience in the quest for it: "And establish the counsel of your own heart, / for no one is more faithful to you than it is. / For a man's soul sometimes keeps him better informed / than seven watchmen sitting high on a watchtower. / And besides all this pray to the Most High / that he may direct your way in truth" (Sir 37:13-15).

In a paradigmatic text, Blaise Pascal (1623-1662) clearly presents the force of reason, both when it doubts and when it accepts its own limitations. What is ultimately at stake is the exercise of freedom, both counseling and allowing oneself to be counseled so as to discern the truth, which Pascal is able to describe with delicate equilibrium (see R. Fisichella, 2014):

We must know where to doubt, where to feel certain, where to submit. He who does not do so understands not the force of reason. There are some who offend against these three rules, either by affirming everything as demonstrative, from want of knowing what demonstration is; or by doubting everything, from want of knowing where to submit; or by submitting in everything, from want of knowing where they must judge. (Pascal, *Pensées*, 268)

If we look at the present time, we can perhaps say what is most urgent is to counsel, provoking questions, in particular questions concerning the meaning of life and the future, "the fundamental questions which pervade human life: *Who am I? Where have I come from and where am I going? Why is there evil? What is there after this life?*" (St. John Paul II, *Fides et Ratio*, 1, emphasis in original).

Instruct the Ignorant

"Do you understand what you are reading?" (Acts 8:30), Philip asks the official reading the prophet Isaiah. And the reply is, "How can I, unless some one guides me?" (v. 31). In the demanding responsibility of guiding and educating consciences, we must remember Jesus' paradigm when he says, "Neither be called masters, for you have one master, the Christ" (Mt 23:10). This includes the confession of faith in Jesus since, "for us there is one God, the Father ... and one Lord, Jesus Christ" (1 Cor 8:6). It definitively highlights the fact that the one who "instructs the ignorant" is Jesus the Messiah, because "whether we live or whether we die, we are the Lord's" (Rom 14:8) (see Ziegenaus, 1997).

In this context, an important and fundamental task arises "to account for the hope that is in you" (1 Pt 3:15). In the encyclical *Fides et Ratio*, St. John Paul II put great stress on this crucial task for our world today when he said, "It is an illusion to think that faith, tied to weak reasoning, might be more penetrating; on the contrary, faith then runs the grave risk of withering into myth or superstition" (48). He concludes that the most urgent task today is "to lead people to discover both their capacity to know the truth and their yearning for the ultimate and definitive meaning of life" (102).

For his part, Pope Francis, in his first apostolic exhortation, *Evangelii Gaudium*, sought to specify the essential points of what the ignorant should be taught about the Christian faith, stressing its "basic core":

> All revealed truths derive from the same divine source and are to be believed with the same faith, yet some of them are more important for giving direct expression to the heart of the Gospel. In this basic core, what shines forth is the beauty of the saving love of God made manifest in Jesus Christ who died and rose from the dead. In this sense, the Second Vatican Council explained, "in Catholic doctrine there exists an order or a 'hierarchy' of truths, since they vary in their relation to the foundation of the Christian faith." This holds true as much for the dogmas of faith as for the whole corpus of the Church's teaching, including her moral teaching. (36)

And a little later he states:

> Just as the organic unity existing among the virtues means that no one of them can be excluded from the Christian ideal, so no truth may be denied. The integrity of the Gospel message must not be deformed. What is more, each truth is better understood when related to the harmonious totality of the Christian message; in this context all of the truths are important and illumine one another. When preaching is faithful to the Gospel, the centrality of certain truths is evident and it becomes

clear that Christian morality is not a form of stoicism, or self-denial, or merely a practical philosophy or a catalogue of sins and faults. Before all else, the Gospel invites us to respond to the God of love who saves us, to see God in others and to go forth from ourselves to seek the good of others. Under no circumstance can this invitation be obscured! (39)

Admonish the Sinner

This is a work of mercy inspired by a classic text of the Gospel of Matthew dealing with conflicts within the community, where the emphasis is shifted from legal thinking to a more ecclesiological and pastoral perspective:

> "If your brother sins against you, go and tell him his fault, between you and him alone. If he listens to you, you have gained your brother. But if he does not listen, take one or two others along with you, that every word may be confirmed by the evidence of two or three witnesses. If he refuses to listen to them, tell it to the Church; and if he refuses to listen even to the Church, let him be to you as a Gentile and a tax collector. (Mt 18:15-17)

The question of fraternal correction is present in the New Testament, and in its use a remarkable realism can be perceived! In this sense, then, it should be noted that correction should be made not as a judgment, but as a service of truth and love, since it addresses the sinner not as an enemy but as a brother (see 2 Thes 3:15). It can thus result in leading a brother who was becoming lost back to life (Jas 5:19).

This fraternal correction is to be exercised firmly (see Ti 1:13), but without harshness (Ps 6:2), without exacerbating or humiliating the one admonished (Eph 6:4). A young person can thus admonish an older person, but with the awareness of his or her condition

(1 Tm 5:1). It is also true that "for the moment all discipline seems painful rather than pleasant; later it yields the peaceful fruit of righteousness to those who have been trained by it" (Heb 12:11).

Fraternal correction requires discernment in order to choose the right moment; to correct so as to increase and not decrease a brother's self-esteem; to exercise it only in truly essential things; to strive to make free rather than to judge and condemn; to correct knowing that you are a sinner and in need of correction. If all this happens, the fraternal correction suggested by "admonish the sinner" may bear the fruit of peace and of blessing (Manicardi).

Having a Conciliatory Spirit

The practice of the following three works favors the conciliatory spirit: comfort the afflicted, forgive offenses willingly, bear wrongs patiently. These three works are part of a conciliatory attitude, a fundamental attribute of a disciple of Christ. We have a conciliatory spirit if we acknowledge our own need to be reconciled to God. Indeed, we cannot comfort, forgive, and patiently endure the injustices unless we recognize that we are debtors to Christ, who continually offers us the way to be reconciled to God (Keeman).

Comfort the Afflicted

In her own history, Jerusalem had the experience of total abandonment. Deprived of all consolation by her allies (see Lam 1:19), she exclaimed, "The LORD has forsaken me, / my Lord has forgotten me" (Is 49:14; see also 54:6-10). But the Lord, in fact, was her real consoler, proclaiming, "Comfort, comfort my people, says your God" (Is 40:1) and "The LORD has comforted his people, / and will have compassion on his afflicted" (Is 49:13).

God indeed comforts his people with the kindness of a shepherd (see Is 40:11; Ps 23:4), the affection of a father, the ardor of a bridegroom and a husband (Is 54), and the tenderness of a mother (Is 66:11-13; 49:15). He has therefore bequeathed to his people his promise (Ps 119:50), his mercy (Ps 119:76), the law and the prophets

(2 Mac 15:9), and Scripture (1 Mac 12:9; Rom 15:4), all of which will allow them to overcome grief and live in hope.

Jesus, announced as the Messiah, "the consolation of Israel" (Lk 2:25), proclaims, "Blessed are those who mourn, for they shall be comforted" (Mt 5:4). He also gives courage to those overwhelmed by sin or by illness, which is a sign of it (see Mt 9:2-22), and offers relief to those who are weary and burdened (Mt 11:28-30).

Paul would later outline the foundations of a Christian theology of consolation in his introduction to the Second Letter to the Corinthians:

> Blessed be the God and Father of our Lord Jesus Christ, the Father of mercies and God of all comfort, who comforts us in all our affliction, so that we may be able to comfort those who are in any affliction, with the comfort with which we ourselves are comforted by God. For as we share abundantly in Christ's sufferings, so through Christ we share abundantly in comfort too. (1:3-5)

Paul also recalls that Christ is the source of all comfort ("encouragement in Christ," Phil 2:1). In the Church, the "consolation" function is essential, since it is a testament to the fact that God permanently comforts the poor and afflicted (see 1 Cor 14:3; Rom 15:5; 2 Cor 7:6; Sir 48:24).

It is significant that the Book of Revelation presents us the moving image of a new heaven and a new earth in which the maximum consolation is that "God will wipe away every tear" (7:17), for "neither shall there be mourning nor crying nor pain any more, for the former things have passed away" (21:4).

Forgive Offenses Willingly

The history of biblical revelation is the story of the revelation of God capable of forgiveness (see Ex 34:6-9; Ps 86:5; 103:3), a claim that entails overcoming the law of retaliation ("eye for eye, tooth for tooth," Ex 21:24) fulfilled in Jesus Christ with his teaching:

> "You have heard that it was said, 'An eye for an eye and a tooth for a tooth.' But I say to you, Do not resist one who is evil.... Love your enemies and pray for those who persecute you.... For if you love those who love you, what reward have you? Do not even the tax collectors do the same?" (Mt 5:38-46)

In this fundamental Christian text Christianity is presented uniquely as an "extreme absolutization" (Luz, 2003) of this love of enemies, present in a generic way in Judaism and some other religions and philosophies (Buddhism, Taoism, India, the Stoic Greek world). The difference with these latter examples lies in the Christian conception of God, manifested vividly in Jesus who acts in a unique way in history. Indeed, the extreme hypothesis of love of enemies corresponds in a special way to the extreme love of God in Jesus, who "having loved his own who were in the world, he loved them to the end" (Jn 13:1).

From a human standpoint the love of the enemies is undeniably Jesus' most demanding requirement, considered since ancient times to be the hallmark of Christian life and conduct. It is a commandment that expresses what is most new and proper to Christianity, since "whoever does not love those who hate him is not Christian" (Second Letter of Clement, 13), and that the love of enemies is a "fundamental law" (Tertullian, *Letter on Patience*, 6) and the "very summit of virtue" (St. John Chrysostom, *Homily on Matthew* 18:4) (see Kasper, 2013).

Thus, for Thomas Aquinas, forgiveness of enemies "belongs to the perfection of charity" (*Summa Theologica*, II-II, Q. 25, Article 8). Hence the importance of forgiveness in order to carry out this act of mercy, well expressed in the Lord's Prayer with the invocation,

"And forgive us our trespasses, / As we forgive those who trespass against us" (Mt 6:12; see also Lk 11:4).

Here too the *Sacrament of Penance* and *Reconciliation* is critical. Pope Francis, in marking the Jubilee Year of Mercy reminds us:

> So many people, including young people, are returning to the Sacrament of Reconciliation.... Let us place the Sacrament of Reconciliation at the center once more in such a way that it will enable people to touch the grandeur of God's mercy with their own hands. For every penitent, it will be a source of true interior peace. I will never tire of insisting that confessors be authentic signs of the Father's mercy. (*Misericordiae Vultus*, 17)

It would be a good idea to recover the intrinsic value of the penitential preparation for the opening rites of the Eucharist, both as an introduction to the Eucharist and as a concrete expression of the sinful condition of the Christian community (see *Lumen Gentium*, 8), when the people of God is directed toward its Lord, recognizing itself a sinner and preparing to welcome God's gift. It is an "act of penance" often attached to the three invocations of the "Lord / Christ / Lord, have mercy" (*Kyrie / Christe / Kyrie, eleison*), in which pastors and faithful together recognize that they are sinners. According to the 1975 version of the General Instruction of the Roman Missal, this involves a dynamic of reconciliation worth highlighting: "Then the priest invites them to take part in the penitential rite, which the entire community carries out through a communal confession and which the priest's absolution brings to an end" (29).

In this context, we can understand why, for the Great Jubilee of 2000, the International Theological Commission published *Memory and Reconciliation: The Church and the Faults of the Past*, in which it explains the ecclesial dimension:

Her "request for pardon must not be understood as an expression of false humility or as a denial of her 2,000-year history, which is certainly rich in merit in the areas of charity, culture, and holiness. Instead she responds to a necessary requirement of the truth, which, in addition to the positive aspects, recognizes the human limitations and weaknesses of the various generations of Christ's disciples." Recognition of the Truth is a source of reconciliation and peace ... the Church "cannot cross the threshold of the new millennium without encouraging her children to purify themselves, through repentance, of past errors and instances of infidelity, inconsistency, and slowness to act. Acknowledging the weaknesses of the past is an act of honesty and courage...." It opens a new tomorrow for everyone." (Conclusion)

Bear Wrongs Patiently

The wisdom tradition forcefully stresses that when faced with irritating brethren, the wise remember: "He who is slow to anger is better than the mighty, / and he who rules his spirit than he who takes a city" (Prv 16:32); "With patience a ruler may be persuaded, / and a soft tongue will break a bone" (Prv 25:15); "Better is the end of a thing than its beginning; / and the patient in spirit is better than the proud in spirit" (Eccl 7:8).

Job is the paradigm of patience: "There was a man in the land of Uz, whose name was Job; and that man was blameless and upright, one who feared God, and turned away from evil" (Jb 1:1), who said, "Naked I came from my mother's womb, and naked shall I return; the Lord gave, and the Lord has taken away; blessed be the name of the Lord" (Jb 1:21). "But he said to her, 'You speak as one of the foolish women would speak. Shall we receive good at the hand of God, and shall we not receive evil?' In all this Job did not sin with his lips" (Jb 2:10).

The Letter of James speaks of the famous patience of Job,

explaining that it is an expression of God's mercy: "Behold, we call those happy who were steadfast. You have heard of the steadfastness of Job, and you have seen the purpose of the Lord, how the Lord is compassionate and merciful" (5:11).

In imitating the patience of Jesus, we see that far from being ruthless with sinners (see Mt 18:23-35), he was tolerant, since our heavenly Father "makes his sun rise on the evil and on the good" (Mt 5:45). This patience, just like love, is a "fruit of the Spirit" (Gal 5:22), mature in trials (Rom 5:3-5; Jas 1:2-4), and generates perseverance and hope that does not disappoint (Rom 5:5). Thus the Pauline hymn of love proclaims that "love is patient" and "bears all things" (1 Cor 13:4, 7).

In this context it should be noted that "patience is an art" (Manicardi). Indeed, to patiently endure in a free and loving way a relationship with someone who is perhaps annoying, unfriendly, boring, sluggish, uncouth, is in line with the love of enemy (see Mt 5:38-48; Lk 6:27-36). And it is also an art when such an attitude encourages reflection on oneself to discover within us that which is also annoying and unbearable for our very selves, and can be also for others, since God in Christ has borne us patiently, loving us unconditionally, reminding us, "Be kind to one another, tenderhearted, forgiving one another, as God in Christ forgave you" (Eph 4:32).

Pray

Pray for the Living and the Dead

As the conclusion to these seven spiritual works of mercy, we present pray for the living and the dead as the synthesis of the earlier works, since prayer is a gift of God in his relationship with man. "Whether we realize it or not, prayer is the encounter of God's thirst with ours. God thirsts that we may thirst for him" (*Catechism of the Catholic Church*, 2560). In short, "Christian prayer is a covenant relationship between God and man in Christ" (*Catechism*, 2564) and therefore sustains all the works of mercy.

There is a thread running through Christian tradition that helps us to understand the meaning of prayer and its relationship to life. It is the famous diptych of the Rule of St. Benedict that has marked all spirituality, not only monastic, but Christian spirituality in general, which says, "pray and work" (*ora et labora*). Following this spirit, St. Ignatius Loyola made it more explicit when he said, "Pray as if everything depended on God and work as if everything depended on you" (see *Catechism*, 2834).

This work of mercy highlights the Communion of Saints in the Church, which is recalled in the Roman Catechism of the sixteenth century: "Whatsoever has been given to the Church is held as a common possession by all her members; to each member of the Church is also assigned his own peculiar office … but all for the common good (cf. 1 Cor 12:23; Eph 4:11)" (I, 9). Ultimately, it is the communion of all of the members of the Church, both those who are pilgrims on earth and the blessed in heaven, who are described as "saints," thanks to their baptism.

The Second Vatican Council described this Communion of Saints this way:

> All in various ways and degrees are in communion in the same charity of God and neighbor.... For all who are in Christ, having his Spirit, form one Church and cleave together in him. Therefore the union of the wayfarers with the brethren who have gone to sleep in the peace of Christ is not in the least weakened or interrupted, but on the contrary, according to the perpetual faith of the Church, is strengthened by communication of spiritual goods. (*Lumen Gentium*, 49)

Thus "if one member endures anything, all the members co-endure it, and if one member is honored, all the members together rejoice" (*Lumen Gentium*, 7).

In this context it is understandable that when we pray for someone living, he or she is placed under the loving and provident gaze of God. God's gift and his blessing are invoked upon that person, so that he or she be sustained on the path of life (see Eph 1:3-14). This does not mean we should necessarily expect concrete fulfillment of all that we ask for, but that through a "specific" request Christian intercessory prayer places every petition within the broader context of Christ's central invocation in the Lord's Prayer, "Thy will be done / On earth as it is in heaven" (Mt 6:10), dramatically repeated by Jesus himself in Gethsemane with an expressive "your will be done" (Mt 26:42).

CONCLUSION

The Works of Mercy: Concrete Testimony of the Preferential Love for the Poor

The formula "preferential love and option for the poor," which is included in a document as universal as the *Catechism of the Catholic Church* and its *Compendium*, sums up beautifully the meaning of the corporal and spiritual works of mercy as a concrete and visible witness of love and the preferential option for the poor. It is a formula that originated particularly on the Latin American continent, and which has been growing and becoming paradigmatic for the entire Catholic Church during the post-conciliar period. For this reason it has been incorporated in the *Catechism*, published in 1992.

In this context, Pope Francis, in his first apostolic exhortation in 2013, strongly consolidated this category by showing that this option and preferential love is not optional for our Church, but is a basic question of the Gospel, since "God shows the poor 'his first mercy' " (*Evangelii Gaudium*, 198). He again mentions this "preferential option for the poorest" in his latest encyclical, *Laudato Si'*, as a significant correlate of the "common good" (158).

In this sense, Pope Francis strongly reiterated in *Evangelii Gaudium*:

> This message is so clear and direct, so simple and eloquent, that no ecclesial interpretation has the right to

relativize it.... This is especially the case with those
biblical exhortations which summon us so forcefully to
brotherly love, to humble and generous service, to justice
and mercy towards the poor. (194)

The pope responds to the question about the more affluent that
are not poor or in marginal situations and how they can live out the
preferential option and love for the poor with the works of mercy.
The answer is taken from a keen, perhaps little known, reflection of
Pope Paul VI, in which he gives decisive guidance for many non-
poor Christians, stating that "the more fortunate should renounce
some of their rights so as to place their goods more generously at
the service of others" (*Evangelii Gaudium*, 190; quoting *Octogesima
Adveniens*, 23).

In this context, Pope Francis dedicates an entire section of
Evangelii Gaudium to the privileged place of the poor in the People
of God (see 197-201) where the word "mercy" appears forcefully:

God's heart has a special place for the poor, so much so
that he himself "became poor" (2 Cor 8:9).... He assured
those burdened by sorrow and crushed by poverty that
God has a special place for them in his heart: "Blessed
are you poor, yours is the kingdom of God" (Lk 6:20);
he made himself one of them: "I was hungry and you
gave me food to eat," and he taught them that mercy
towards all of these is the key to heaven (cf. Mt 25:5ff.)

For the Church, the option for the poor is primarily a
theological category rather than a cultural, sociological,
political, or philosophical one. God shows the poor "his
first mercy." This divine preference has consequences for
the faith life of all Christians, since we are called to have
"this mind ... which was in Jesus Christ" (Phil 2:5).
Inspired by this, the Church has made an option for the
poor which is understood as a "special form of primacy

in the exercise of Christian charity, to which the whole tradition of the Church bears witness." This option — as Benedict XVI has taught — "is implicit in our Christian faith in a God who became poor for us, so as to enrich us with his poverty." This is why I want a Church which is poor and for the poor.... We are called to find Christ in them, to lend our voice to their causes, but also to be their friends, to listen to them, to speak for them, and to embrace the mysterious wisdom which God wishes to share with us through them. (197-198)

This option and preferential love for the poor involves a perception and understanding of the different kinds of poverty to which the corporal and spiritual works of mercy refer.

The Four Kinds of Poverty That Correspond to the Works of Mercy

It can be observed that the listing of the fourteen works of mercy — seven corporal and seven spiritual — corresponds to four kinds of poverty (Kasper, 2013). The most basic is *physical*, or economic, poverty, such as having no food or drink to satisfy hunger and thirst, no roof, no clothes, no shelter, to which could be added unemployment and serious illnesses or disabilities. This poverty is attested to in the first, second, third, and fourth corporal works of mercy.

Physical poverty is followed by *cultural* poverty, with illiteracy at its root, along with the absence and lack of educational opportunities, and, ultimately, the lack of a future with the social and cultural exclusion it carries. This poverty is met by the first, second, and third spiritual works of mercy. A third form is the *social and relational*, from solitude and withdrawal, the death of a spouse, the death of family members and close friends, external and internal difficulties of social communication of all kinds, discrimination and marginalization, to isolation by imprisonment and exile. This poverty is present in the corporal works of mercy — the fifth, sixth, and seventh — and in the spiritual — the fifth and sixth. Finally, there is *spiritual* poverty, such as disorientation, inner emptiness, distress, and even despair about the meaning of one's own existence, moral and spiritual confusion, self-abandonment, the absence or marginalization of the religious dimension, apathy or overwhelming indifference. This poverty is attested to especially in the fourth and seventh spiritual works of mercy.

Obviously, the corporal and spiritual works of mercy need cross-fertilization. In fact, the material support understood in the corporal works is fundamental for *physical poverty*, but Christian mercy entails also alleviating the *cultural*, *social*, and *spiritual poverty* that the spiritual works of mercy address. All of this is to enable the person in need not to remain in a permanent state of dependency, but to progressively become a "help for self-help" (Kasper). Hence the importance of a comprehensive approach to the works of mercy that is cognizant of the different dimensions of poverty.

The Works of Mercy as Something More than Justice

We should note that neither the corporal works of mercy, nor particularly the spiritual, reference commandments of God's law, as happens with the six works of merciful love in Last Judgment discourse of Matthew 25, in which there is no condemnation for sinners who have violated any of the commandments. Jesus' condemnation is instead addressed to the omission of good — what are classically called "sins of omission" — since the point is to act with the greatest amount of justice. As Jesus said in the Sermon on the Mount: "Unless your righteousness exceeds that of the scribes and Pharisees, you will never enter the kingdom of heaven" (Mt 5:20).

This "greater justice" proposed in Matthew's Sermon on the Mount is not merely a quantitative intensification of life before God, but a qualitative one, since it is not purely a more detailed compliance with the law but is realized in terms of self-giving and service in the image of God's "extreme love" manifested in Jesus Christ ("He loved them to the end," Jn 13:1). For this reason, we can sin by omission regarding this love for the poor and needy, since mercy transcends justice, giving full attention and generous love, being, in turn, more radically sensitive to and in solidarity with of all kinds of poverty and marginalization. This is the understanding expressed by Pope Francis when he wrote, "Mercy is not opposed to justice but rather expresses God's way of reaching out to the sinner, offering him a new chance to look at himself, convert, and believe" (*Misericordiae Vultus*, 21).

As Pope Benedict XVI taught:

> Love — *caritas* — will always prove necessary, even in the most just society. There is no ordering of the State so just that it can eliminate the need for a service of love. Whoever wants to eliminate love is preparing to eliminate man as such. There will always be suffering which cries out for consolation and help. There will always be loneliness. There will always be situations of material need where help in the form of concrete love of neighbor is indispensable. (*Deus Caritas Est*, 28)

The reflection on the corporal and spiritual works of mercy for the Jubilee, according to Pope Francis, "will be a way to reawaken our conscience, too often grown dull in the face of poverty. And let us enter more deeply into the heart of the Gospel where the poor have a special experience of God's mercy" (*Misericordiae Vultus*, 15).

Mary, Mother of Mercy

A careful reading of the stories of the Annunciation (see Lk 1:26-38) and the canticle of the *Magnificat*, which expressly refers to "mercy" (Lk 1:46-55), together with the wedding feast at Cana (Jn 2:1-12) and the scene of Mary at the foot of the cross (Jn 19:26) offers a beautiful biblical compendium of the action of divine mercy in Mary, which can strongly illuminate the realization of both the corporal and spiritual works of mercy in this Jubilee Year.

We can also remember with joy that in one of the most famous hymns to Mary, the *Salve Regina* (eleventh century), she is invoked as "Mother of Mercy." Moreover, in the litanies of the Rosary (twelfth century) she is remembered as "Mother of Divine Grace," "Health of the Sick," "Comforter of the Afflicted," and "Help of Christians," expressions that explicitly recall the works of mercy.

We conclude with the final wish of Pope Francis:

> May the sweetness of her countenance watch over us in this Holy Year, so that all of us may rediscover the joy of God's tenderness. No one has penetrated the profound mystery of the incarnation like Mary. Her entire life was patterned after the presence of mercy made flesh. The Mother of the Crucified and Risen One has entered the sanctuary of divine mercy because she participated intimately in the mystery of his love. (*Misericordiae Vultus*, 24)

BIBLIOGRAPHY

Callahan, Sidney. *With All Our Heart and Mind. The Spiritual Works of Mercy in a Psychological Age*, Crossroad, New York, 1988.

Davies, W.D., and Allison, Dale C. *The Gospel According to Saint Matthew III*, Clark, Edinburg, 1988, 416-434 ("The Judgement of the Son of Man: 25.31-46").

Gielen, Marlis, and Bopp, Karl. "Werke der Barmherzigkeit," *LTK* 10 (2001) 1098-1100.

Gomá, Isidro. *El Evangelio según san Mateo (14-28)*, Marova, Madrid, 1976, 569-592 (Mt 25:31-46).

Gray, Sherman W. *The Least of My Brothers: Matthew 25:31-46. A History of Interpretation*, Scholars Press, Atlanta, 1989.

Grün, Anselm. *Damit Welt verwandelt wird. Die sieben Werke der Barmherzigkeit*, Gütersloher, München, 2008 [= *Perché il mondo sia trasformato. Le sette opere di misericordia*, Queriniana, Brescia, 2009].

Kasper, Walter. *La misericordia. Clave del Evangelio y de la vida cristiana*, Sal Terrae, Santander, 2013, 140-143 (*"La obras corporales y espirituales de misericordia"*).

Keenan, James F. *The Works of Mercy. The Heart of Catholicism*, Pastoral Center, Lanham, 2008 [= *Le opere di misericordia. Cuore del cristianesimo*, EDB, Bologna, 2010].

Léon-Dufour, Xavier (ed.). *Vocabulario de Teología Bíblica*, Herder, Barcelona, 1972.

Luz, Ulrich. *El Evangelio según san Mateo III (1997)*. Sígueme, Salamanca, 2003, 659-696 (Mt 25:31-46).

Manicardi, Luciano. *La fatica de la Carità*. Qiqajon, Bosé, 2010, 55-198 (*Le opere di misericordia*).

———. *Le opere di misericordia*, Ed. CVS, Roma, 2009.

Militello, Cetina. *Le opere di misericordia*, San Paolo, Milano, 2012.

Noble, H-D. "Notes et appendices." *Saint Thomas d'Aquin, Somme Théologique, La Charité*, *2ª-2ª, Questions 27-33*, Desclée, Paris, 1942, 115-127.310-315 [q. 32, aa. 2-3].

Noye, Irénee. "*Miséricorde (Oeuvres de)*." *DSp* X (1980) 1328-1349.

Pié-Ninot, Salvador. *Eclesiología*, Sígueme, Salamanca, 2015, 202-203 ("*sacramento del hermano*") [= *Ecclesiologia*, Queriniana, Brescia, 2008, 214-215].

Royo Marín, Antonio. "Virtud y obras de misericordia," *GER* XVI (1973) 14-17.

Scaraffia, Lucetta. (ed.), *Le opere di misericordia spirituale*, Messaggero, Padova, 2014 (authors: R. Fisichella; C. Aubin; M.M. Zuppi; F. Coccopalmerio; G. C. Bregantini; G. Pasquale; R. Boccardo).

Ziegenaus, Anton. *Die geistigen Werke der Barmherzigkeit*, Johannes-Verlag, Leutesdorf, 1997.